Printed in Great Britain
by Amazon

Malcolm Johnson; August 1994

EARTHQUAKE
and other poems

Also by Lotte Kramer

Ice Break *(Annakinn)*
Family Arrivals *(Poet and Printer)*
A Lifelong House *(Hippopotamus Press)*
The Shoemaker's Wife *(Hippopotamus Press)*
The Desecration of Trees *(Hippopotamus Press)*

Lotte Kramer

EARTHQUAKE
and other poems

Rockingham Press

Published in 1994
by
The Rockingham Press
11 Musley Lane,
Ware, Herts
SG12 7EN

Copyright © Lotte Kramer, 1994

British Library Cataloguing-in-Publication Data

A catalogue record for this book
is available from the British Library

ISBN 1 873468 23 7

Printed in Great Britain
by Bemrose Shafron (Printers) Ltd,
Chester

Printed on Recycled Paper

For Nat

'There is no harder prison than writing verse,
what's poetry, if it is worth its salt,
but a phrase men can pass from hand to mouth?'

Derek Walcott *(Forest of Europe)*

ACKNOWLEDGEMENTS

Some of the following poems appeared first in Acumen, Agenda, Ambit, Ariel (Canada), Assegai, Chapman, The Christian Science Monitor, Country Life, The Countryman, John Clare Society Journal, 'Chaos of the Night' (Virago), 'Criminal Records' (Viking Penguin), European Judaism, Festschrift for Edward Lowbury, The Jewish Chronicle, The Jewish Quarterly, The Month, Other Poetry, Outposts Quarterly, PEN International, Poetry Durham, Proof, Quartz, The Rialto, Samphire, New Spokes, Tribune, The Spectator, Ver Poets, 'Vision On' and Writing Women.

CONTENTS

JANUARY	9
POWER CUT	10
EARTHQUAKE	11
DEAD RHINE	12
JOURNEY	13
JUDGEMENT	13
THE FALL	14
BEETHOVEN AND I	15
A NEW SUBJECT	16
PREMONITION	17
TWO COUSINS	18
HUNGER	20
BIRTHDAY POEM FOR MY MOTHER	21
A FABLE	22
CISSIE	23
TWO GREAT AUNTS	24
A PAIR OF SPECTACLES	25
CENTRAL CEMETERY, VIENNA	26
SURVIVOR	27
POST-WAR I	28
POST-WAR II	28
POST-WAR III	29
POST-WAR IV	29
POST-WAR V	30
POST-WAR VI	31
THE SOUND OF ROOTS	32
DIRGE	33
COCOON	34
HOMESICK	35
WEDDING POEM	36
CELEBRATION	37
AGEING FEMALE FAUST	38
ON BREAKING DOWN THE BERLIN WALL	39
IMMIGRANTS	39
DUEL	40
FEAST DAY IN SIENA	41
GHIRLANDAIO'S 'LAST SUPPER'	42
IN SALZBURG	43

TOO MUCH OF EDEN	*44*
WIND AND GRANADA	*45*
1492 — 1992	*46*
DIALOGUE WITH UTRILLO	*47*
AROSA VOICES	*48*
THE LONELINESS OF AN EMPTY RAILWAY CARRIAGE	*51*
TRAIN JOURNEY TO ELY	*52*
THE BAIT OF LIGHT	*53*
STRAWBERRY PICKING	*54*
IN SOUTHEY WOOD	*55*
LIGHT	*56*
BEFORE NIGHT	*57*
SEESAW	*58*
STONE WOMAN	*59*
LANE AT LONGTHORPE	*60*
THE CHESTNUT TREES' COMPLAINT	*61*
LABURNUM	*62*
INSTINCT	*63*
FOR COLETTE	*64*
THRESHOLDS	*65*
AFTER SEEING THE EDVARD MUNCH PAINTINGS	*66*
KÄTHE KOLLWITZ (THE SURVIVORS 1923)	*67*
AFTER THE THEATRE	*68*
BREAKING THE RULES	*69*
MUTE	*70*
MARRIAGE VOWS	*71*
AT A LECTURE	*72*
ASSOCIATION	*72*
THE MOTH	*73*
IN US THE HILLS	*74*
NOW	*74*
CONTACT	*75*
HAIKU	*75*
BETWEEN MOON AND SUNSET	*76*
DREAM YOKE	*77*
NEXUS	*78*
THE OLD FOUNTAIN (Carossa)	*79*
THE DEATH OF MOSES (Rilke)	*80*

JANUARY

White and stiff,
A frozen mask,
Janus guards the new gate.

Only he
Can lick last year's wounds
With one side of his tongue

While not
One creature returns
From the old side of the fence,

Not one hand
Can prevent or caution
Words of a twelvemonth.

He hears
Cold certainty
For thirty-one days

Yet his face
Turns surprise ready
In a thaw of newness.

POWER CUT

Suddenly the television died
That late Sunday afternoon
When dusk threatened into dark:

Unused to shadowless silence
I hunt for candles
Stowed away for years

In some understair hold;
Distant 'safe rooms'
Plugged against poison.

I bleed white wax into saucers
On the kitchen table,
Huddle by the gas oven's lit throat

And read flickering words
Of poems that leap up
In triumph over this muteness.

From our cavern I watch
How blackness intensifies
Punctured by flashlights of cars

As we slide deeper into night
With its blur and footsteps,
Take comfort in uncertainty

Of the almost limbo
Where loss congregates
On the far side of sleep

Until, in an explosion of light
Noises intrude and demand
The deep-freeze whines again.

EARTHQUAKE

'Please save my brother, he's still there' he said
Clutching his pen, wearing his pin-stripe suit
Though dust and mortar stiffened him to lead.

The rubble falling round him and his head
Dizzy and bleeding. 'I'm an accountant,
 Please save my brother, he's still there' he said.

It took six seconds for the earth to shed
Her mother image and destroy its root
When dust and mortar stiffened him to lead.

Too few can crawl to safety from their bed,
Escape the knock at dawn, the vicious boot.
'Please save my brother, he's still there' he said.

Pompeii choked. No time for wine and bread.
Vesuvius boiled and strangled every street.
The dust and mortar stiffened him to lead.

We walk away from craters, feel instead
Some kind of grief for one whose world is mute.
'Please save my brother, he's still there' he said
Though dust and mortar stiffened him to lead.

DEAD RHINE

That river cannot weep,
Poison has starched his eyes
To a witches' frost of sleep.

Where once, a child, I slipped
Into his soft green silk
And loved the slimy steps

That led me down, now stand
The mourners coffin-deep
Watching the dry-eyed land

Lament a dark disease
That from some human hands
Flung devils to the trees,

To waters and their beasts.
Oh plunge your fists through fears
And find a ring that keeps

Tenure and faith with tears.

*Note: people were mourning in this way
when toxic waste poisoned the river*

JOURNEY

Around us
The earth of my bones
Knowing me
Better than any other;
Sand in my blood
Edging the Rhine's centuries,
My life's river
Kneeling at the town's cobbles,
Watering
The reddening sins,
The sprouting
Memories of snakes
Licking away fire
With their quick tongues.

JUDGEMENT

You, who have not walked
Through the blurred edge of my Hades,
Who have never been dwarfed
By insisting clinkers of spent flames,
Who look not for a name
In anonymous ashes —
Do not encapsulate
A judgement or eavesdrop on pain,
But learn to move
In the flux of a stranger's veins
Over mountains
And from room to room.

THE FALL

She kneels on soft sand,
Keeps washing her hands,
Again and again
In the lake,

Loves the cool wetness
Creating patterns
That slither and split-off
In rings,

Is often amazed
To find herself faced
By the bed-room mirror
Person:

The child with her name
Her nurse had explained
Holding her up
To cold glass;

She tries to touch her,
Nearly can reach her — when
Blackness is slapping
Her face ...

BEETHOVEN AND I

for Edward Lowbury

He sat white, brooding, on the piano top.
We were on speaking terms, I knew him well,
But as a sleepy child at night I could not
Tolerate the sounds his music made.

I'd cry and beg for it to cease, my hands
Over my ears. His anger, passion, pain,
Disturbed and hurt. I could not understand
His tense assault nor my response to it.

But in the day I'd sit for hours listening
Under the piano, humming with that voice:
Sonatas, Lieder, spilling down their notes
Into my private shelter, touching light.

At night I only wanted simpleness,
The near-death distances of silent dark.

A NEW SUBJECT

'Today we start a subject that is new
To everyone. As your new master now
I've come to tell you something of those true
Great ancestors we have. You must be proud,

You boys, our fatherland, our new decade,
Is nurtured by a giant race: red-blond,
Eyes blue, a strong physique and unafraid.
The finest ethnic heritage is ours.

Let's see the type of man we used to be —
Yes you — just there — behind that darkish head,
You in the seventh row — get up, come here!
What is your name? Ah, Heinz, ah, very good.

Now face the class. You see in this blond boy
The perfect specimen of purest race;
His bones are powerful, his hair is fair,
His eyes are blue set in an eager face.

No shameful mixture in his blood or breed.
This is your future now, our Germany!
You grin — you laugh — you too — I'll have no cheek
From anyone! What is the matter, speak?'

'Please Sir, it makes no sense, it's true, you see
Heinz is a Jew.'

PREMONITION

Late afternoon
In a darkening room,
A girl alone.

Outside, the streetlamps,
Lakes of shadows
And hollow footsteps.

On her desk her homework,
Additions, fractions,
Clinging to black ink;

She cannot forge
Cohesive answers
As the night collects.

She feels its menace
Invade each space
In prophetic trance,

And terror as huge
As unexplained mountains
Oppress the minutes.

Fears for her mother's
Unusual absence,
Her orphaned lostness

Are tangible omens
In time's reversals
And future nightmares.

TWO COUSINS

I

The Rhineland summer hung
On cobble stones;
They threw down satchels, rushed
Where water seams
The edge of sand and grass.

They loved the slimy steps
That led them down
Into green wetness, silk
Cooling their limbs,
Dividing swiftness, glass.

Strength against strength, the river
Will demand their
Dipping, stretching dance
To force collusion,
Join his hunger for the sea.

II

Later, in nine-year old
Carnality
They'd face a mirror, look
For family traits,
Searching identities:

> "You're like your mother, small
> And dark, features
> The same" one cousin said,
> "But I am blond,
> Blue-eyed, and not at all

>Like anyone." They puzzled
Long and hard, then
Fell into a happy
Resolution:
>>"You're like your grandmother,

>>Her face is just as square,
>>Although her hair
>>Is white now, you're like her!"
So satisfied
They pinned down certainties.

III

Outside the race-laws ravaged families.
Their school was burnt, became a burial ground
For all their carefree fun, their playfulness.

One day they heard the adults' whispered words:
'Adoption, separation, kidnapped life'
And even threat of prison haunted sleep,

Sent them to different corners of the globe.
"You know, my birthplace was not in this town",
She tried this confidence before she left.

>"My mother was a young girl in Berlin,
>I don't know who my father was ..."
The other one pretended not to hear.

HUNGER

"Hunger,
Loud and visible,
Hung like heavy
Harness round our necks
And never let us breathe —
And yet when bread
Was allocated
Dirty hands would fetch
The loaves pressed
To arms and coats
Where lice and fleas
Kept house. I wiped it
With a cloth — then
I ate."

BIRTHDAY POEM FOR MY MOTHER

Today I have reached the year of your dying.
Again I bleed with your limitless falling.

In your enduring is night of beginning
To measure the unsure dawn of each morning.

You laboured to give me light we call living;
Your torment denied the untempered journey.

There is no redemption in slender offering,
Help me to kneel in the desert of weakness:

Only a moment from Sinai's glowing,
Only a husk of an unsponsored answer.

There is no frontier to losing and healing,
My coming-of-age breaks on summits of praying

Now in this autumn that taught me my breathing,
Appled and auburn with your first blood's promise.

A FABLE

That time
When the 'Final Solution'
Became known as the unacceptable fact

You sat
In front of me on an English bus:
The back of your head, your hair, your skin,

The way
The nape of your neck with its small
Dark point moved from side to side

In cautious
Rhythm, the slightly helpless
Expression of your thin shoulders ...

The shock
Shivered through me like fire.
Seconds of fabled seeing until

The other
Woman with the stranger's face
Turned round to get off at the next stop.

CISSIE

Her name was Cissie
And she mangled sheets,
Her hair was peroxide yellow;
She crooned about love
With a smoker's cough
While the sweat slipped down her belly.
She could tell a tale
Full of sex and ale
As the mangle wheeled her story,
And her laughter roared
As her bosom soared
When she slapped the sheets to glory.
In a war-time pub
Some G.I. pick-up
Cheered the Monday morning queues,
But below her pride
Of the good-time night
Were a lonely woman's blues.
For once in a while
A black eye would smile
From her puffy face full of sweat;
And we knew it meant
Her old man had spent
The infrequent night in her bed.
So she rolled and roared
As she laughed and whored
Till one day she clocked-in no more:
No G.I. or mate
Kept her out so late —
But a Buzz-bomb had struck her door.

TWO GREAT AUNTS

Aunt Bertha and Aunt Sarah
Lived in unharmony
Devoted to each other
Through wars of jealousy.

Two sisters, widowed early,
They shared a cosy nook,
Aunt B., the younger of the two,
Was housekeeper and cook

And trotted to the market
Quite early in the day,
She was a match for any rogue
And quick-tongued in a fray.

More serious was Aunt Sarah,
More on her dignity;
She queened it from her armchair
With an arthritic knee

She'd covered with a cat's fur,
She stroked it with a sigh
Expecting homage as her due
From all the family.

She got it — and was much esteemed
As regal to the core —
Aunt Bertha twinkled, took
Herself out through the kitchen door.

She ended up in Canada,
Miles from her native Rhine.
Aunt Sarah bitterly survived
A Nazi camp near Spain

And sat out years in USA
Complaining that her son
Had taken on second wife
Without her blessing given.

A PAIR OF SPECTACLES

He sent his spectacles without a word.
His farewell letter, silent, unexplained.
Just safely padded and the gilt frame shone
Round eyeless lenses. So much care had gone
Into this packaging. Two women held
The glass and metal in their hands and wept

Grief on this morning proof. For days they'd kept
On hoping he'd come home. They had been told
Of some discrepancy at work, finance
He'd dealt with. Not like him to bank on chance.
No swindler he — a decent Catholic
Who loved his life, his family, liked a drink
And music, played the organ in the church —
The postman brought a shame they could not touch.

CENTRAL CEMETERY, VIENNA

'Gate four' you asked,
The woman flinched
But then pointed the way.

And so we entered
Through the Jewish Gate
To find the silent density

Of graves. The one
You looked for, near
Some fallen stones, still

Upright, barely
Readable and overgrown.
'Johanna Spinka 1852-1935'.

The grandmother,
Agile and small. A boy,
You filled her false-teeth cup

With onion rings.
You pinched the cakes
She baked before she died.

A good age then,
Not like that evil time
When plots stayed empty here.

Now only names
Commemorate
These absences where trees

Throw shadows
Over tortured script,
Over the patient grass.

SURVIVOR

for Anita Lasker-Wallfisch, cellist

It was the cello
Saved her life.
That giant bass
Stood waiting
For her hands,
For her to underwrite
The marchers at the gate,
To ease their tread,
Their great fatigue,
To watch them fall.

Her sixteen years,
A study-store of loss,
Still taught her how
To draw the bow
Across the gut of grief,
Transmute
That evil time
Into some russet
Sounds of warmth,
Some notes of hope.

POST-WAR I

Time was, when for the price of 1/6
We'd go to the pictures, saw the B-one first,
Trailer, the news, and then the main big fix;
My hanky at the ready for a burst
Of damp emotion. Three hours at least
Of therapeutic wallow kept us sane
In that post-war austerity, a boost,
After a day of tooling the machine
For you, or sweating at a laundry
Calendar, for me, with aching back
And legs. This was our weekly luxury.
Then we'd walk home to our two rooms; with luck
There was a shilling for the gas. The loo,
The bath, were shared, the dripping geyser too.

POST-WAR II

Then I'd rush home at night and look for mail
From Europe, via the Red Cross, maybe,
To say my parents had been traced, though frail
And ill but still alive ... a dream for me

And many others. A sterile make-belief
That led to nightmares, split my mind. The days
Were filled with slogging work. I buried grief,
Hunted for rations, joined banana queues.

Now looking back from years they never reached
I wonder who she was, this person 'I'
Who rushed up the bare stair-boards that we shared

With other tenants in the house. I try
Pursuing her into our two-room flat
And will not find that letter on the mat.

POST-WAR III

There was a queue for everything, bananas,
Oranges, when they appeared, and even
Waiting lists for dining tables, chairs,
All of the one utility design.

We got our things in dribs and drabs, a special
Favour every time. Bread was still rationed,
So were meat, sugar and tea. And fuel
Was in short supply. When we were visited

Friends brought their rations as a gift. One winter,
When it was particularly cold,
The pints of milk were ice on doorsteps, water
Froze in tank and pipes, and then it thawed:

We woke to floods bursting through ceiling, wall,
And had to camp out in our draughty hall.

POST-WAR IV

Then came the news from France of who'd survived
From all the family. Just one or two
By a mere thread or miracle returned
From hell to shadow those whose names caused too

Much pain remembering. And when we met
Again for the first time, below the joy
Were tales untold or only hinted at.
They'd walked on quicksand through a human lie.

We could not know a fraction of their fears.
Our trauma had been statelessness and war
That branded us as aliens in those years
When we were allies really from before

Hostilities. Our lives could not compare
With those dark memories that they could not share.

POST-WAR V

Your letter, searching for me, crossed with mine
Searching for you. My 'Wahlverwandtschaft' older
Sister in enemy country. Not one sign
Of bitterness. Knowing of bombs and fire

Where we used to play and fearing for your
Life so many times, to see your writing
On the envelope crossed grief with joy. For
Now you told me how you fled still carting

Those mementos that my mother brought at dawn,
Her curfew visits, how you saved your child,
Your mother too. But war had meant destruction
Of our town, and worst: had felled your husband.

In those first letters we nailed down our tales
Of you as widow, I as orphan, balanced scales.

POST-WAR VI

In France there was some heirloom jewellery,
Smuggled and hidden in the Nazi years,
Now found again and mostly ownerless.
It crouched inside my palm as family

Survivor. I recognised the bracelet
And the ring, Victorian brooches set in
Filigree with weeping rubies. Secret
Histories escaping in a tin

From gas and ash, divorced from neck and arm,
The warmth that cradled them in Kaiser's time
Or later in the 20s decadence.
Now, in the island's twilight, life or chance

On certain days will bring these items out
To give them air, to mourn, to celebrate.

THE SOUND OF ROOTS

You remember more each day
Of language, people and town.
You have returned, a long way
From the burdened child to this sound

Of the whispering roots: "Come near",
They say, "Shed you fear, turn your
Janus head and see how far
And deep we can stretch through the years

Through the centuries in this soil.
We moved with the Rhine, knew the Roman
Yoke, the crusaders' cruel toil.
Yet we harbour here where wine

Grows strong, where we still belong,
Do you hear?" Yes, you listen
And let the blindfold fall from
Your stranger's eyes and you mourn.

DIRGE

i.m. Karen Gershon, 1923 — 1993

You now at peace
From our ancient restlessness
Shatter my grief
At the numbness of worlds.

Ahead of me, always,
You told our black song.
I share that tune
Till the end of my story.

The printed line,
The pebble I bring to you
To set on your grave,
To surrender my sorrow.

Like spring's giant shadow
Blotting the fence,
You fled from the sun
That jewels new grass.

Your words ignited
From streets of fire
Return to the pool
In childhood's mirror.

COCOON

She says she can't remember anything
Of people, language, town; not even school
Where we were classmates. Her smile is frail
And hides behind her husband's hypnotising

Quietness. 'A Suffolk man' he beams,
And squares his tweedy frame against some
Unseen advocates who might still claim
An inch of her. She is content, it seems,

To lose her early childhood; he is near.
Protector or destroyer, it's his war.
He underwrites her willed amnesia,
Helps her to stifle terror, exile, fear.

She is cocooned, safe as an English wife,
Never to split that shell and crawl through love.

HOMESICK

Still the same search for home.
Not a return,
Nor familiarity,
But the once-known
Threshold of otherness.

Years wipe away
Your fingermarks. Your chair
Is too clean; too
Much light waits in this room;
These curtains fall

Together pointlessly.
Other voices
Carpet the stairs, picture
A wall, a nail
Curls against their colours,

Breaks inside me.
I must look for a place
Without echoes:
Hope will breed in a bed
Of hopelessness.

WEDDING POEM

for Stephen and Miriam

The substance that has made you from my flesh
Now satisfies the chapter of your youth.

Today my paragraph means 'letting go'
As mothers always learn the time of turning.

From that old wind of deserts now I pray
For a new innocence, a view of wonder,

To occupy your mutual travelling,
So hungry eyes may summon colour, light,

To temperate the dark. There will be shadows
You must touch and fight with hardened hands.

But always name and praise the opulence
Of living — make alien wind your own.

CELEBRATION

To celebrate the house
They built the roof

And with the roof's completion
Came the child

And in her hands she held
The sapling tree

The tree with coloured ribbons
In the wind

And in the wind she moved
With careful steps

Along the planks
That led up to the height

The gabled height
Where stood the cheering men

And cheers were guiding her
From all around

Till she had brought it safely
To the peak

And on the peak they fixed
The ribboned tree

And baptised it with brandy
Glass by glass

To celebrate the roof
The house... the child...

AGEING FEMALE FAUST

Before her final descent
She is practising deep-sea diving
Exploring the liquid extremeties
Of that eau-de-nil world.

Mephisto is still patient;
Knowing she cannot escape him
He permits her limbs' agility
In candelabra of movements.

He fosters her blood's marathon
Penetrating her veins in all directions
To taste origins and juvenilia
Of earthly continents.

Her memory refuses to acknowledge
His grip on her earlier achievements,
His hand in her creative sign
Is now blurred alchemy in her eyes.

Charon can wait as well
Certain of his cargo across the Styx.
Then she'll be reunited with the devil's
Most efficient favourite.

ON BREAKING DOWN THE BERLIN WALL

"The new meat is eaten with the old forks."
                              Bertolt Brecht (New Ages)

And they
Who never knew
The fat meat of freedom,
The strong beer of liberty,
Are filled
With bright magnesium
Of exploration:
May they use it
With the knowledge
Of wise doctors.

IMMIGRANTS

The wolves are coming back to Germany.
Across the Polish border
Barricades are down:
The wolves slink into forests in the dark

And bring a darker Russia in their veins.
They sniff out ancient fairy tales
Trading in omens, hunger, fear,
Looking for hidden spaces under rocks.

At night they cluster by the edge of woods
In families of threes and fours,
Howling their wail of loneliness
Over the Eastern villages and plains.

DUEL

Returning again from the other side
                 of the Channel,
My two languages are running a race
                 in my head.
One, from the depth of watery childhood
                 by the Rhine
Is insisting on its prerogative place,
                 undermining
The second one's well-shaped resourcefulness,
                 its everyday use.
This battle is as ancient and familiar as
                 my ageing skin,
As my now tired feet that have met
                 the old cobblestones
Round the Dom, have crushed the sand
                 framing the river.
'Return to clay soil' I command and face
                 the flat land,
My adoptive earth. It will take time
                 for purified words
To assemble in their bastion of isolation.

FEAST DAY IN SIENA

Our guide speaks broken English laced with garlic.
Her white umbrella waves above the crowd
And all her words dance on a spiral sound.

The shell-shaped, peopled piazza speaks in stones.
The famous pink-burnt colour climbs the sky
With towers, roofs, breaking into the blue.

This is a town for people, cobbles shout.
In the self-service restaurant a fat
Mamma peels a courgette and shares it out

Among her family — including us —
Insisting that we eat it too! The loo
Is a stampede, a female storm, no queue!

It is St. Catherine's birthday and we pass
Her house, all flowers; yard and balcony
In copper stone and brick. The zebra-striped

Cathedral sits above the rest. Too many
Shoes have split that inlaid marble floor;
We step on stories under covers now

Except one roped-off square where guides outshout
Each other in confusion, splendour, noise,
Until we face the Duccio, calm and wise.

GHIRLANDAIO'S 'LAST SUPPER'

(San Ognissanti, Florence)

We rush out early
Past the oily Arno
To savour silence
In the cloister's stone,
A brown monk only
Guarding guides and cards.

Confronting us those
Talking men at supper
That last, much painted one.
We enter, eavesdrop, see:
A frame of lemon trees,
A blue-white cloth
The table's gentle shroud
Or else protection
From some menace here.

Clusters of cherries
Gleam like promises
And distant birds tell
Of some new perspective
Bringing completeness
To each living sound.

IN SALZBURG

In the morning,
At the Markartplatz,
Leopold Mozart sends
A thousand kisses home
And Wolfgang complains
Of his sore behind
From the long coach-ride
To Mannheim.
His concertante sings.

At midday,
The thoughtful face
Of Stefan Zweig
Astonishes the trees
On the Kapuzinerberg.
That sad exile
Stays all afternoon,
Walks to the courtyard,
The room where Georg Trakl
Pours words of terror
And beauty on our century.

TOO MUCH OF EDEN

What says the Seine at night?
Towers and bridges soar in too much light,

Too much of Eden drowns and daubs the dark,
Water will not defend itself. The bark

Of circus boats, the glare
Reflecting eyes that shun the neon stare

Looking for silence on a further bank,
Taking us down to islands lapped in ink.

WIND AND GRANADA

I

Language of olive trees,
Silver in the wind
From the Sierra Nevada
Across hills and valleys
Where iron adds drama
To mountain pleats:
A knife of red paint
In white sandy soil.
Untidy groups
Of brown goats tumble
Over rocks by the wayside
Where Lorca has captured
That hot afternoon.

II

Again the wind on the hill
Of the red fortress.
In the sunny courtyard
Fountains and flowers
Echo filigree arches;
The twelve lions,
The tribes of Israel,
Exuding heat as ancient
As their white stone
From before Isabella
Decreed our expulsion;
In the gardens the cypresses
Protect our walk.

1492 — 1992

Who remembers our expulsion
From that apricot land?
Who remembers our flames
At the stake on refusal
To recant or accept
That man-God they said
Yahweh sent?

In Isabella's hands
We lost our neighbours,
Our Muslim friends,
Our poets and doctors,
Our flowered doorways
To terraces, gardens.

Who sings of our fountains:
The lions of Judah
Carved in white stone,
Now in a courtyard
Sparkling in exile
And alien wind?

DIALOGUE WITH UTRILLO

A white street in Montmartre
On a Swiss hotel room wall,
With steps leading up steeply.

Some shutters closed against heat
As I shut mine today after
Coming down from the mountain.

A lamp-post in that street keeps faith
With silence of long-gowned figures
Singly climbing the hill,

A promise of leaf-cool trees
At the top where shade collects
The midday in a small square.

Here, the evening light yellows
The rocks below the glacier,
Gathering in their loneliness;

And three cows announce themselves
Belling along the village street
Led by a girl in red jeans.

AROSA VOICES

I View

Sunlight on rocks
Twinning shadows
With endurance.
Valley illusions
Pointing at contours
That zigzag the sky.
Distant voices,
The woodcutters rasp
Marries the wind.

II The Lake's Riddle

The lake has its own language.
It gives back absolutes:
Trees, houses, humans.
When a boat tries to fathom
Its centre, no sounds break
The oars' coaching and slapping
Of the water's feminine hunger.
Light can decipher it more easily
Penetrating below the green surface
Or feeding clouds as shadows
To the mirror of its waves. So it will be
When we lie on the other side of the riddle.

III The Trees' Certainty

Trees are the old certainties.
I look into them, smell their scent,
Breathe in the faith of childhood.
When sun lightens their branches
Stars drip their silent glitter
On the path where pine needles crackle,
Dark roots knot themselves in clusters,
A different haunting hammers answers:
They know of sickness and world sorrow,
Are martyrs to the air's poison
But still stand erect in their sureness.

IV Meadows

The meadows are the mothers of us all.
No chairlift can destroy their welcome,
Juicy with wild flowers and fat grass.
They know the edge of existence
Where the treeline begins, but their valleys
Continue for ever. Even concrete
Can't destroy them. They'll be there again
Long after our houses have crumbled,
Shrouding the much-tortured earth.

V Zauberberg

Here, on the 'Zauberberg'
In walls surrounded by trees
And mountains
That bend in evening sun,
We breathe the air
That could not save
So many from dying.
Here, the magician
Sat and wrote,
Snatching a flame
From the lives of his puppets
Who loved and talked
On the slopes of this greenness.
Hans Carstorp
Lies on his long chair
Looking into the night
Until his existence
Tumbles into our century's lottery.

THE LONELINESS OF AN EMPTY RAILWAY CARRIAGE

The city dirt,
The sharp smell of burnt oil,
Hang on this train;

Empty and swept
It slides its old-fashioned rump
Through the greening night;

From a tall nail
A long yellow sheet
Rocks in its plastic jive,

The floors are cold
With dull mosaics
Of permanent stains.

No other life
Shares in this carriage ride
With me,

While I watch
In the dusk the closing in
Of bereaved upholstery,

Knowing there's light
Somewhere outside
Where a table is laid,

Or where cattle stand
With good faces
In the mist of a spring meadow.

TRAIN JOURNEY TO ELY

It seems as if the tall, expressive grasses
                      had a say
In this calm plain. This landscape hides its drama,
                      hardly moves
From my slow train, yet dominates the sky
                      or else there is
A marriage with the obdurate horizon
                      where the mist
Performs its rite. The corn is still unharvested,
                      it shines almost
To spite the clouds; and as we draw into the red-
                      brick station
The engine drums the sound of afternoon.
                      Yet underneath
The waters move; a secrecy; the endless
                      reservoir
That's camouflaged with soil and grass and grain
                      and has a pact
With skies. And nothing burns now, as on other
                      days, when sun
Intensifies all that the earth has yielded
                      and its pain.

THE BAIT OF LIGHT

In the quiet selection of words
A sun-blinded bird
Crashed against my glass.

It lay numbed on the stone-path,
His flight's abrupt end
Cutting my poem from its root.

That other time, when waiting
For your arrival, a sparrow
Mistook my window for light

But survived the impact enough
For a brief hop on the grass before flight.
A good omen — I thought then.

Now, an old woman stands plumbed
Into soil at the crossroads,
Staring into the sunset.—

'How beautiful' she hums in her
Asthmatic voice, her face a young
Reflection, her eyes dance.

STRAWBERRY PICKING

We become stooping pincers
Greedy for the red fruit,

The juices oil us from all sides
As we search under leaves,

Birds and slugs have carved their fill
Leaving wounds,

Rain and mud have taken their toll
In ferment and mould

Spreading sick-white wool,
Denting flesh,

And still we race in a fever
Of success and hunger

Filling baskets, ignoring
The spikes in our backs,

Stemming briefly the ripening
Fungi in ourselves,

Knowing the new proximity
Of next year's harvest.

IN SOUTHEY WOOD

Trees with moss feet
Grow upright in this wood.

Their trunks articulate
And carved as pain

Still dominate in league
With umber light.

A reassurance
After storms when rust

And timber coat
The path soon to ferment

And feed the earth.
This hunger, where we stand

In clumps of clay,
Protects and knows

The limit of our walk,
The borderline of grief.

LIGHT

On the edge of water
Light is gathered
To draw you in,
To invade you.

Darkness surrenders
To visions of feeling,
To deepened space
In lucent glass.

A world as real
As the netted moon
With a million stars
In a captured dome.

BEFORE NIGHT

November dusk discolours
Minute by minute,
Pulling out landmarks
Like teeth, leaving
The lake's mouth
Awash with silence.

The eye's arrow
Hits a triangular buoy
That still brags its red
Identity. But the fierce
Night will swallow it too.
Trees survive longest:

Those dark signposts
Pleading, stretching
Arms to the East
And West, to the North
Away from their roots
Saying: 'Save us!'

SEESAW

At school,
On the other side of the Channel,
I was taught
Oliver Cromwell was a hero,
A man of vision.

In England,
Living with an upper-crust family,
Democracy
In peril during the 2nd World War,
He was a villain.

But now,
In his native countryside
Near the Great Ouse,
The smashed cathedral glass
Receives the white light

Of the fens.
There is a sense of independence
In that black earth
Sponsoring his army of footsteps
All the way to the gallows.

STONE WOMAN

(Grafham Church)

I cannot rise again
But am content
To stretch my wind-bleached
Body on the grass,
To open up my belly
For the few that need
My darkness.

Here it is good
To listen to the lake
As it repeats its sea-sad
Tune all through the year.

My eyes echo
The sun and watch
The earth relent each spring.
I relish kinship
With the trees. They guard
My loneliness, the quiet
That I hold and pour
Into some thirsty throats.

Those that have made me
Loved my Northern skin
So much, they carved it
With their ornaments,
Their myths, condemned
My roots to motherhood.

LANE AT LONGTHORPE

Enter the lane:
A long pale tongue
Licking the Green

Where the old barn
Cages bull and cows
Manuring the air.

An armful of trees
Dribbling and roofing
The path, arching

From hedge to hedge
With bramble and hawthorn
As weathervanes, each

For their separate seasons.
Here every month
Is a mouthful,

A feast of vegetable
Silence —
Art Nouveau repeating itself.

THE CHESTNUT TREES' COMPLAINT

We stand green-garbed and candle-lit
Unmoving on the village green,
Two giant aunts that arm in arm
Review the altered spring-cleaned scene:

This docile housing now in place
Of cattle, mud, and where at times
A fierce black tethered bull had stormed
His tiny green circumference.

And where the barn had slightly leant
On elderly, substantial stones
We see suburban gardens bloom
Too neat, without the cow-dung smells.

All used to pleasure, flatter us.
Still in our density we glow
Down to our ankles, thick as cream,
Proud unforgetting in each flame.

LABURNUM

(Goldregen)

Laburnum,
'Golden rain',
Housed in the many gardens
I have known,
Brother of
Lilac,
Spill yellow softness
On my lawn, bring
Down and spread
Brightness
Of sun,
The ever friendship
Of each spring.

INSTINCT

That summer in the heat
We saw an old man,
Watering can in hand,
Bend over anxiously,
Soaking a door-mat on the ground.

'Keeping it moist'
He then explained,
'Will help to nurture
 Food for birds,
 Breed worms and insects underneath

 To keep their young alive
 For the next season.'
Too often lately we had seen
Some tiny fledgling
Dead on pavements.

Some said, the parents,
Helpless in the drought,
Had rather pushed them
From the nest
Than watch them starve!

FOR COLETTE

Through her
I take possession
Of that long, hard gaze
To know
The scarlet pulse in men,
In plants, in animals,
To tell
The charm and misery
Of us: in love with love,
To hear
In summer's alphabet
The earth-voice of a mother
To melt
The yeast of memories,
Touch with my palm, my tongue,
My shin
Each unmet thought and taste,
Inhabit houses, new
At first,
Inherit libraries
Alive with dust and smell,
Declare
The movement of each limb
As pleasure's miracle.

THRESHOLDS

Three girls on a bridge, Edvard Munch

Dusk — a promise of dawn.
We cross a bridge
Where three girls
Are leaning
On the edge of childhood
And wooden railings.
They bend
In a half-way house
Of future fears
Only their hair
Streams backwards
With the wind's will.
They stare
At the river's journey
Of forests and cities,
Of light before light.

AFTER SEEING THE EDVARD MUNCH PAINTINGS

Everything pales:
Too grey the polished night,
Brass chains in the black Thames,
Rust hair on the girl's head.
Too still:
The train's thud on the bridge.
No red more scarlet than
His distance, her hands, his ears,
The edge
Where sanity melts, where
Consolation is fear
And love the muscle of war.
In him:
Birth leans on the steep bridge
Of dying, hugs the flood's knife
For ever. Colour and line
Cry out
His blood's soliloquy,
His hell's message —
As we must walk over the bridge.

KÄTHE KOLLWITZ
(THE SURVIVORS 1923)

These angular passions
Of black and white
Are streaming with colours,

Uprights of hunger
Down to the marrow
Of bones and eyes,

Arms that embrace
Declensions of death
With iron frontiers,

She, the mother,
Roofing her hands
That cleanse and thunder

Year after year
Through the wrong silence
To the cloudburst: man

AFTER THE THEATRE

Brimful with words.
St. Paul's blooming down-river,
Hungerford bridge a chain
Across the Thames whose purse
Opens with teeth of lights.

But curled in corners,
In cardboard, in silence,
The smell of L-and-S-shaped
Heaps of the homeless —
In this nursery of pleasure.

Again, at the escalator's base,
Someone sharing the ground
With rats and mice.
A green youth kneels down
To press a coin into that old fist.

BREAKING THE RULES

Markets and figures shape the afternoon.
Minutes are moved,
The chairman's voice bores on,
Shareholders concentrate.

Only one old man weeps
His swan-song from the board,
His stick a gong of drumming emphasis,
Body a pendulum, lament in every bone:

"No one before me
 Has yet had to resign!"
The family hums on:
Another year is straddled on a nephew's back

And soon outsiders
Will return the ride.
He'll stay director
Of the rawness of his pain.

The May sun fractures
Light with grief as plain as ageing,
A clan of merchants
Breaks the rules of graves.

MUTE

'I stabbed that woman
Right into her heart
And slashed her through and through

Across the gold and blueness
Of her vest, her cloak, her hands,
Her baby too —

But then they whistled,
Gripped my arms,
I felt the strain invade my neck,

Was led through halls
Of multitudes
Where none would hear

That I had come to her
A thousand times,
Had begged for recognition,

Warmth, had craved
A wife, a child, a home
Out of the winter rain!

That muteness stung me
To despair, so on this day
I took a knife to her for all to see.

Only I wonder
Why there was no blood.
My cell is warm and dry.'

*Note: a man was apprehended for slashing a painting
in a gallery.*

MARRIAGE VOWS

(Observations from the back of a church)

All through the marriage vows
He looked at her with bitter eyes,
Assertive as the law,
While she stood, face averted,
Shoulders shrinking with each word,
Tears on her book.

How much, for whom, they really cared
Inside their fashionable clothes,
Was hard to tell.
Something was still alive enough
To hurt the camouflage
Of make-belief.

And all the time
Still pledging,
Young and new,
Those others stood
Before the priest
Like sentinels.

AT A LECTURE

Such sadness
Grained in that man's face.
Again and again,
Like a hungry sin,
My eyes bridged
The gangway to his grief
Eavesdropping against my will
At the door
Of his bearded plea.

ASSOCIATION

First week into
The New Year
A smudge of orange peel
Squats in the lane.

A sun-set stain
In a mud-sky
As casual as
Wind-blown hair
On a lover's head,
Turning.

THE MOTH

Evening time when the roses walk
Away from the fence, out of the leaves,
Glowing their crimson, yellow and white
Virginities through dusk. Wind has ceased.
And the word 'summer' travels the air
That is peopled with smells and sounds of night.
In the distance a streetlamp shatters a tree,
The motorway's noise is a cradle-song
For the orphan day, For the infant light.

Say that this moth is a thought returned,
Voice of a face that knows its lack
Stabbing persistence into the dark:
Word without answer, name without word,
Creature of half-light calling me back.

IN US THE HILLS

In us the hills
Remember absolutes.
We hold a truth
Larger than vows, larger
Than life or loss.
A child needs promises
To trust the years
But hills in us belie
Those patient fields
Where space outlives your eye's
Incessant search.

NOW

You tell me not to say 'the last'
Of anything:
Of walks, of places, views,
But to regard
Each time as now, as always.
That looking back
Denotes no loss, no sadness,
When to-morrow's change
Will emphasize those yesterdays:
The stones we find,
The pine-cones with their weather charts,
The dried wild marjoram,
All stress your bright philosophy —
As treeless earth
That celebrates the wind.

CONTACT

I'll keep this green cone
With the faint cedar scent,
A candle you plucked
From the tree as I left.

The resin wept down
Its pineapple curve
And sealed our hands
With the glue of its sap.

Now lustre still clings
To the side that I touch,
Feel the soft liquid purge
Our spiral of years.

HAIKU

Today,
In my pensioner's year,
I envied the paper
In your hand.

BETWEEN MOON AND SUNSET

In August
Before dusk
My house sits
Between Moon and sunset:

Ceramic O
Almost full
Stands crusted
In its own order

Facing hot
Copper lines
That broaden
And blur

From the oozing
Sun. With the last
Daylight
A briefness

Transmutes
The minute's
Movement
Between seeing and losing

To new hours
That will reach
You in time
With visible thoughts.

DREAM YOKE

My shoulders ache
From the mud-weight of autumn,

My hair is shorn
By the edge of its rage,

My eyelids lose
The elastic of water,

My hands cannot rest
From the milk of its moon;

My legs are locked
In the granite of laughter,

I fall from the sun
To the round bruise of day,

I wake in my sheets
As a hamster of freedom.

NEXUS

When young,
I used to blame the old ones
For their make-belief world,
For their refusal to meet fears
Or hurl stones at the sky.

Years later,
I find myself on their stage,
The same curtains drawn
In a charade of blind-man's-buff
As an ostrich struts through sand.

THE OLD FOUNTAIN

after Hans Carossa

Put out you light and sleep! Only the splashing
Sound here of the old and ever-wakeful fountain.
But every single guest who had been resting
Under my roof has got accustomed to it soon.

It may be, though, that when you are already
Dreaming, a restlessness walks round the house,
The gravel grates with steps that seem so heavy,
The fountain's splashing stops, a sudden pause.

And you wake up — must not be startled then!
The stars are standing all above the land,
Only a wanderer at the marble basin
Scoops water in the hollow of his hand.

He'll go soon and the rushing sounds at night
As always; be glad you won't stay lonely here.
Many are wandering far under the starlight,
And many, on their way to you, draw near.

THE DEATH OF MOSES

after Rainer Maria Rilke

No one, only the dark fallen angel
wanted it; took weapons, entered the death
of the assigned. But again and again
he crashed backwards, upwards,
cried to the heavens: I cannot!

Because calmly, through the brow's thicket,
Moses had perceived him and carried on writing:
words of blessing and the unending name.
And his eye remained pure to the ground of strength.

Then the Lord, tearing with him half the skies,
surged down and made up the mountain bed himself;
bedded the old man. From the ordered dwelling
he called for the soul; she arose! and told of
much that was shared, an infinite friendship.

But in the end it was enough for her. She, made whole,
admitted it should be enough. So the old God
bowed his old face slowly towards the old man.
Took him from his old age with a kiss
into his own, older one. And with hands of creation
he covered the mountain. So that there should be only
the one, re-created, among the mountains of the earth,
unknown to mankind.